Is Mejor to say ADIÓS

Alondra Delgado

Copyright © 2022 Alondra Delgado

All rights reserved.

ISBN: 979-8-218-03389-7

"Para esos que han sufrido por amor. Ese que duele, ese que es verdadero. Que tus lágrimas no aparten el rayo de luz que tú mismo produces. No dejes que un corazón roto, rompa la esencia de quien realmente eres. Tú puedes levantarte. Tú has vivido de verdad."

CONTENTS

1   Primera Parte   1

     Poemas en Español

2   Part 2   Pg #44

     Poems in English

ACKNOWLEDGMENTS

Ever since I was seven years old I would write poems about love without even knowing what it was. Over the years the thought of love changed drastically. Through good and bad relationships, family, and friendships, I discovered that love wasn't a fairy tale like they portray it in movies. Love is real and it's not easy. But it is so much more. I still think that real love is unstoppable and capable of everything but I do think we settle a lot and do not give ourselves the chance to be loved the right way. I want to say thank you to those who have shown me what love is. Big thanks to my mom who loves me and my brother unconditionally. That is the kind of love that fuels me to be better. I wouldn't be where I am without her. To my whole family my brother, my dad, my grandparents, aunt, and uncles, thank you. Your love and support has motivate me to be better in life and this is for you. Cheers to my first book! It is a dream come true.

SIN MARCHA ATRÁS

"Me fui porque merecía más.

Me alejé porque no me querías.

Me hice la fuerte ocultando lo que sentía,

y tú ni insististe por explicar tus mentiras.

Te dije adiós con dolor en el alma.

Me fui retirando con mucha calma.

Me volteé a mirarte despacio,

pero ya entre los dos, era muy grande el espacio.

Entonces comprendí mi error.

Nunca debí abrir mi corazón.

Pues mientras te amaba sin control,

tú me destruías sin compasión."

TUS OJOS

"Dicen que los ojos no mienten.

Pero no sé qué pasa con los míos,

que piden a gritos amor

y tú, que los miras de cerca,

ni les prestas atención."

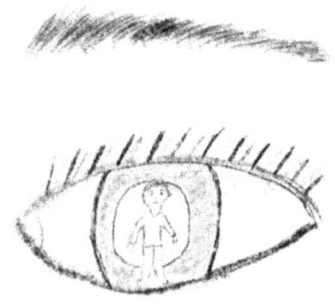

NI MÁS NI MENOS

"No pido más ni menos.

Pues menos tiempo sería nada

y más tiempo no me deja extrañarte.

Pido justo lo que tenemos, pero constante.

Que te tenga en mi vida

y sienta las ansias de amarte."

DECIDE

"Me elevas...

me llevas a las nubes

y luego me bajas.

Me das falsas ilusiones

y al rato me matas.

Ya estoy cansada de este sube y baja.

Si estás es para quedarte.

Pero me cansé de suplicarte.

Así que decide por favor,

pues quiero saber

si tengo que amarte u odiarte."

VUELVE

"Te dije que te fueras

sin pensar que te fueras a ir.

Ahora me encuentro sola

buscando razones para vivir.

Me dejaste en el vacío

y ahora cada día se siente más frío.

Vuelve a mi te lo pido,

pues mi vida sin ti no tiene sentido."

AUN

"Aún te miro.

Aún te deseo.

Aún te regalo una sonrisa.

Aún te ofrezco mi ayuda cuando la necesitas.

Aún quiero hablarte.

Aún me gustaría besarte.

Aún quisiera abrazarte.

Y es que aún me quedan ganas de amarte."

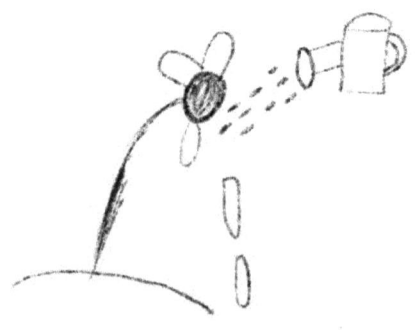

ME DISTE LO PEOR

"Me diste lo peor manipulándome a pensar que era

lo mejor. ¿Sexo rápido en el carro?

¡Qué divertido! ¿Cero caballerismo?

¡Qué moderno! ¿Celos incontrolables?

¡Qué mucho le importo!

Mientras yo te daba todo,

tú me dabas lo peor.

Y aun así cuando yo decidí irme,

me culpaste con rencor.

Entonces, yo sentí que fallaba;

Cuando sólo fui una víctima más

a quien supiste engañar, en darme lo que tal vez

 al momento necesitaba, pero no merecía.

Me diste lo peor, pero ya nunca más

aceptaré menos de lo mejor."

ENTENDI

"Tropecé con muchas montañas.

Caí enredada en telarañas.

Me usaron sin yo querer.

Me mentí a mí misma y me equivoqué.

Hice cosas que me arrepiento.

Fui inepta y cuánto lo siento.

Ignoré las señales

y me alejé de tus mares.

Pero al fin y al cabo,

después de todos esos malos pasos,

tú no te diste por vencido

y regresaste a mi vida con un motivo.

Después de tanto tiempo,

 veo la importancia de este trayecto.

Entendí que nadie me ama como me amas,

y no hay felicidad más pura que estar cara a cara."

CULPABLE DE MI PENA

"Sabía que esto iba a pasar.

Me meto en cosas que al final no voy a tolerar.

Digo que sí.

Digo tal vez.

Para luego querer hacer las cosas al revés.

Me encierro yo misma

en una calle sin salida.

Y ahora finjo algo,

que sólo fue una falsa ilusión,

que me confundió por un rato."

ASI DE FACIL

"Así de fácil, así de simple,

ya no somos los mismos.

Nos ganó la monotonía,

se suicidó la libertad,

desapareció la honestidad.

El tiempo y la distancia

fueron más que el amor

y ganó la ignorancia.

Así de rápido, así de triste.

Dejamos que las conversaciones

se convirtieran en peleas

y las palabras en falsas promesas.

Así de fácil, así de simple,

perdemos poco a poco un amor

que con respeto y dedicación

crecería día a día sin control."

DESESPERACIÓN

"Desesperación…

es lo que siento yo.

Por el desconocimiento;

Por el sufrimiento de mi pueblo.

Mi patria, ay, mi alma!

Qué dolor profundo yo tengo.

Mi isla bella, mi tierra del encanto,

cuánto te amo y te extraño.

Somos fuerte, somos uno

y de esta haremos un triunfo.

No me quito, no me canso.

Pues un jíbaro verdadero, lucha sin descanso.

Puerto Rico se levantará

y de esta, más brillará.

Porque no hay huracán María,

que destruya el espíritu de la patria más linda."

TE FUISTE TU

"Te fuiste tú...

y tal vez yo mucho no luché.

Pero te fuiste tú...

Y a lo mejor yo en varias cosas fallé,

Pero te fuiste tú...

Y quizás yo no expresé cuanto te amé,

Pero te fuiste tú...

Y si te extraño yo, ¿qué hago?

¿Espero a que regreses tú o me marcho yo?

Te fuiste tú...

Y ahora ya es muy tarde para explicarte:

que te fuiste tú, pero yo a la vez me fui.

Me perdí en mí misma y sigo buscándote a ti.

Te fuiste tú. Y me obligaste a irme a mí,

a olvidarte a propósito, para poder sobrevivir.

Te fuiste tú. Y cuánto quisiera que aún estuvieses aquí."

SEGURO SUICIDIO

"Y mi corazón parpadeará,

y mi mente viajará,

y mis manos temblarán,

cuando escuche tu nombre.

No importa el tiempo,

No importan los años,

Tu recuerdo siempre me hará daño.

Es dulce, es amargo,

Y me destruye sin pensarlo.

No fuiste el amor de mi vida,

fuiste quien me cambió sin medida.

Pero qué importa cuánto haya sufrido,

si cuando la vida te trae de nuevo,

escojo el seguro suicidio."

TU RECUERDO

"Claro está, te extraño.

Es imposible negarlo.

Me haces falta, te lo juro.

Día a día vivo en un luto.

Recuerdo los buenos tiempos y sufro en silencio.

Pero sonrío y continuo.

Pues tú estás mejor y eso, te lo aseguro.

Mi vida ya es distinta,

tal vez menos divertida.

Pero me aferro a tu sonrisa,

y eso, me da vida.

Vivo de tu recuerdo,

y aunque desearía que fuese cierto,

la memoria de tu amor,

me da fuerza en momentos perfectos."

SE CANSÓ

"Y se cansó de tus mentiras.

Y se acostumbró a tus desilusiones.

Y te miró definida.

Y se marchó sin confusiones."

JAMÁS

"Te amó, te perdonó.

Se cansó y te olvidó.

Ahora aguanta presión,

pues jamás encontrarás comparación."

EN UNA NOCHE FRIA

"Aquí en una noche fría me encuentro vacía.

Buscando las respuestas a tantas preguntas.

Tratando de entender lo que no tiene sentido,

lo que no vale la pena.

Vacía por decisión propia,

por no aprender en cabeza ajena.

En noches frías como estas,

tú me calentabas y ahora, ya no estas.

Tengo que aprender que cada cual tiene calor propio.

Y cada cual es completo.

No te debo de necesitar para calentarme

o completarme.

La noche está muy fría.

Pero ya mi alma se cansó de enfriarse.

Es tiempo de cambiar.

Es tiempo de olvidarte."

DOS LOCOS ENAMORADOS

"Y yo sé.

Sé que lo nuestro no funcionó.

Y que tal vez si lo volvamos a intentar, no funcionará.

Pero me haces falta, te echo de menos.

Te pienso en las mañanas, te sueño despierto.

Te extraño en cada momento.

Es difícil desear a alguien que no te merece.

Querer estar con quien más te hiere.

Pero al final y al cabo,

siempre hemos sido dos locos enamorados,

expertos en hacerse daño."

MUJER MALVADA

"Me puse celosa no porque sea insegura,

sino porque la carne es débil y la mujer es malvada.

Sabemos cómo manipular y conseguir lo que queremos.

El hombre cae por tentación

y nosotras ganamos la atención.

Cuando dije que estaba celosa,

no es que no confíe en ti.

Es que estoy segura de lo que soy capaz yo.

Estoy celosa de que ella logre lo que pude hacer yo.

Y te pierda a ti, por un negativo don."

NO ME QUERIA IR

"Es cierto, tal vez yo me fui.

Pero me fui porque ya tú no eras el mismo.

Me quería quedar, pero me tuve que ir.

Y desde ese día, quiero volver.

Volver a sentirme cerca, a tenerte conmigo.

Pero tú te fuiste por definido.

Y aunque me gustaría pensar que al igual que yo,

quieres volver, sé que estés donde estés

celebras que al fin estás bien.

Y sé que por tu parte, no quieres volver.

Querías que me fuera cuando me fui,

y no quieres que vuelva,

pero sin ti no quiero seguir."

ME HIERES

"Y entonces, ¿vas a ser igual que todos?

¿Me usarás e ilusionarás para luego negarme?

No, yo creo que eres peor que los otros.

Me llamas amor, me agarras la mano,

me llevas siempre a tu lado.

Para que cuando te confronten,

¿te avergüences y me niegues?

Me hieres, sí me hieres...

Y yo creyéndome la mentira de que me quieres."

UNA NOCHE ETERNA

"Quiero una noche contigo.

No de esas que pasan y se olvidan.

Una noche que nos una de por vida.

Una noche donde tus manos tomen las mías

y tú abrazo arrope mi vida.

Quiero respirar tu mismo aire.

Quiero sentir tu calor. Quiero conocerte.

Que no haga falta quitarse la ropa

para que exista conexión.

Quiero que me hagas el amor con palabras,

con miradas. Que lentamente la noche nos una

y seamos uno. Quiero una noche eterna.

De esas que solo existen en películas.

Que tu pecho sea mi almohada,

que tus besos sanen mis penas.

Una noche para la historia

porque así de mucho significas"

MI CUERPO

"Mi cuerpo no es un premio.

No es algo que luchas por conseguir

 y luego dejas colgado en la coqueta de tu cuarto.

No soy un objeto temporero que se deja utilizar

a tu manera y a tu tiempo.

Mi cuerpo tiene alma, mi cuerpo tiene vida.

Si deseo darte mi cuerpo es decisión mía,

es porque yo quiero. Y si aún no lo has tenido,

es porque sé que valgo más que eso.

Hombres como tú,

tienen juguetes ya designados para ellos.

Hombres como tú,

no merecen un ser humano envuelto en su juego.

Mi cuerpo no es un premio.

Y si fuera así, no te lo ganaste."

NO SOY UNA OPCION

"Entonces, ¿qué pensabas?

¿Que con ambas podías jugar?

¿Que sería divertido tener dos o tres?

O tal vez pensabas, que ¿te iba a perdonar?

Que ¿te iba a esperar? Que podías tomar el tiempo

necesario para tomar una decisión.

Pero, cariño, ¿se te olvida algo?

Yo no tengo que esperar a que alguien decida,

 porque yo no soy una opción.

Si para ti soy una entre muchas,

tú para mi serás del montón.

Ya quítate ese papel de víctima confundida

que ama a dos a la misma vez.

Eso no funciona conmigo.

Creo que ambos sabemos tu decisión,

Y esa, es decirme adiós."

LA VIDA

"Ayer una dama me dijo:

"Te ves triste, ¿qué te pasa?"

Varias cosas han pasado en estos últimos años.

(Digo en mi mente)

"Eso es que lo extrañas" me vuelve a hablar la dama.

"No, no es eso". Le contesto.

La sociedad tiene una mala percepción.

La felicidad de una persona no es determinada por

la soledad o la compañía.

Uno es feliz consigo mismo, o se supone que así sea.

No le expliqué las razones a aquella dama

porque no sentía la necesidad de explicar

mi estado emocional.

Pero aquí hoy escribo y me desahogo.

La vida te da cantazos de los que caes y te levantas

y algunos te hacen caer más bajo que otros.

Esa es la razón de mi mirada triste, la vida."

NO ES TAN SIMPLE

"Odio la idea y la imagen que las personas tienen

respecto al sexo hoy en día.

¡Qué vulgar, qué feo!

¡Qué simple, qué insignificante!

¿Acaso se les olvida que literalmente dos cuerpos

se unen en el acto?

¿Acaso se les olvida que la mujer está dejando entrar

parte de tu ser en ella?

Es uno de los actos más íntimos y delicados

que pueden existir.

Y ahora, hoy en día, sexo es sexo.

Ya ni importancia tiene. No hay pasión.

Pero es mucho más que eso.

Tal vez deberíamos volver a aprender sobre el tema."

IDENTIDAD

"Vivimos en una sociedad donde el tema de identidad

se ha vuelto una confusión.

Como mujer quiero igualdad y respeto.

Pero a la vez quiero alguien que me ame,

respete y me proteja.

Quiero ser independiente pero me gustaría

un hombre que me cuide y ayude.

Entonces la sociedad nos confunde.

Para ser una mujer independiente y 'bichota'

no necesitamos un hombre que nos controle.

Pero eso no es lo que queremos. O lo que yo quiero.

Quiero ser una mujer independiente que quiere

la ayuda y opinión de su pareja de igual manera

que él quiera la mía.

Ayuda no es debilidad.

Una relación es un equipo y tal vez debemos empezar

a ver a la mujer y el hombre como un equipo

y no una competencia a ser igual que el otro.

Quiero un hombre que me dé espacio a ser libre

y el chance de ser fuerte y débil a la misma vez.

No quiero ser el alfa, solo quiero ser.

A veces es difícil ser mujer."

POR QUE

"A veces aún escucho tu nombre.

Me levanta en las noches.

Pero siempre aparecen sólo los buenos recuerdos.

Los momentos de sonrisas y caricias.

¿Por qué se me hace tan difícil pensar en los malos?

Esos momentos donde mentías

y me faltabas el respeto.

¿Por qué se me hace tan difícil olvidarte?

Si ya no estás y jamás volverás.

¿Por qué mi corazón no puede odiarte?"

EN ESA BARRA

"¿Crees que no puedo oler el olor a flores

y tequila en tu cuerpo?

¿Quién ha estado besando tu cuello?

¿En qué barra? ¿En qué pueblo?

¿Es mejor que yo?

¿Es más atractiva?

Preguntas y preguntas circulan mi mente.

Pero jamás me dirás. De eso sí estoy segura.

Entonces, ¿me quedo con la duda?

¿Será esta tu única?

Creo que ni tú ni yo creemos eso.

Entonces, sé hombre y dime la verdad.

Cuéntame como todos los jueves te vas a disfrutar

mientras me llamas en el baño contándome

cómo la pasas de lo más padre con tus "amigos".

Y yo me quedo en la casa como tú me adviertes,

mientras mis amigas salen a la misma barra

donde te ven con la tipa esa.

"Te están mintiendo." "Yo jamás haría eso."

La próxima semana te veo allí en esa barra,

pero soltera.

Ahora a mí me toca disfrutar.

No me llames más."

YO SÍ ME AMO A MÍ

"Qué difícil es amar a alguien que no se ama

a él mismo.

Por más que tratas y tratas,

todo pasa por desapercibido.

Todo es mi culpa, todo es por mí.

El alcohol es su mejor amigo y de 7 días,

tal vez 2 de la semana se acuerda que estoy aquí.

Al próximo día después de la resaca, yo soy buena.

Soy la mejor novia del mundo que cuida por ti.

Pero la noche anterior te importó madres

cuando le pegaste a la pared y yo por miedo

decidí quedarme a dormir en el piso del baño.

Porque por alguna razón aquel piso frío y duro

se sentía mejor que compartir una cama contigo.

Me cansé de fingir. No te puedo obligar

a encontrarte a ti. Si no me amas, déjame ir.

Yo sí me amo a mí y por eso, me voy de aquí."

SIN TI

"Me cansé.

Me cansé de aparentar, de mentir.

Quiero ser real, quiero sonreír.

La realidad es que no soy feliz.

Honestamente,

necesito estar sin tí."

¿AMOR U OBSESIÓN?

"Y ahora vuelves otra vez.

Y yo me vuelvo a perder.

Nuevamente, mi mundo al revés,

me pongo a tus pies.

Y me pregunto.

¿Es esto amor?

¿Es este sentimiento que duele y mata tranquilidad?

¿Es esta necesidad de tenerte cerca libertad?

Necesito una señal,

saber cómo reaccionar,

a esta llegada agria,

llena de confusión y aparente felicidad."

POCO A POCO

"Si lo sé, me duele.

Si lo sé, me quema.

Si lo sé, muero por dentro.

Si lo sé, sobreviviré."

PREFIERO SI TE QUEDAS

"Si te vas no me muero.

No es que sin ti no pueda vivir.

Pero si te quedas, sería más vida.

Y mucho más divertida.

Así que no te vayas,

y tengamos lo mejor de los días."

TEN METAS

"Hay una diferencia entre los sueños y las metas.

Existen quienes sólo sueñan en grande

y quienes se sacrifican por su gran carrera."

NECESIDAD

"El sexo con otro es como la comida.

Aunque no te guste, llega el momento

que te estas muriendo

y te la tienes que comer."

UNA Y OTRA VEZ

"Un chicle viejo en tu boca es como una relación tóxica.

Aunque ya no tenga sabor,

lo sigues masticando."

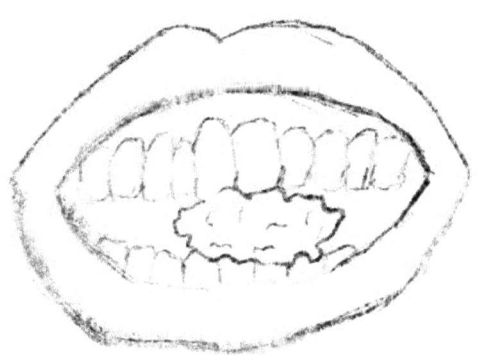

MENTIRAS

"Me decías te amo mientras besabas a otra.

Me decías que era la única,

mientras te enredabas en sus sábanas.

Me celabas.

¡Qué mucho me celabas!

Para que al final del día me enterara

que tu inseguridad era fruto de tu infidelidad.

Y tus besos y te amos,

eran mentiras para usarme por tan sólo un rato."

FINGIAS

"Y me miraste y me abrazaste.

Y me tocaste y me besaste.

Y me tomaste de la mano

Y caminaste a mi lado.

Me hiciste feliz.

Y luego te marchaste de repente

y me dejaste fríamente.

 Sin un adiós,

sin un perdón.

Supiste engañarme.

Hacerme creer que era algo especial,

cuando para ti, todo era superficial."

UNA ÚLTIMA CARTA PARA VOS

Fuiste el primer hombre a quien amé.
Después de ti, cada hombre en mi vida
ha sido un intento en vano,
en buscar tu reflejo en algún lado.
Me enseñaste a amar a tu manera.
A creer en mí y ser libre
y no prisionera.
Pero de igual manera,
de ti también aprendí algunas debilidades
e inseguridades.
Aprendí a ser terca
y sólo ver las cosas como yo quiera.
Y hoy que ya no estás me doy cuenta,
que tal vez no necesito buscar en cada hombre tu reflejo.
Porque nadie va a ser como tú.
Pero jamás imaginé que aun siendo tú,
te fueras y me dejaras sola a mí.
Mi primer amor,
te llevaste la mitad de mi corazón.
Mi capricornio favorito,
jamás entenderé la razón, pero hoy te digo:
Ya te perdoné.
Espero que algún día tú puedas hacer lo mismo.

Con amor siempre,
      Lola María.

Is Mejor to say ADIOS

Is Mejor to say ADIOS

PART 2

Is Mejor to say ADIOS

"For those who have been in love. The kind of love that hurts, the one that kills. I hope you know, it'll get better. It has to. And to my exes. Trust me, I wouldn't be writing this book without you. Literally. Heart break made me stronger and made me value who I am today. So, thank you, I guess."

WHEN I LEFT

"When I left, you didn't care.

When I left, you didn't notice.

When I left, it didn't hurt you,

because you made sure I was the only one loving.

It was never you."

SOBER NOW

"I've been a month clean.

Clean of the drug that fucks me up.

The drug that made me be a different person.

That drug that made me love myself

and hate me so much.

The drug that made me feel so high and so down.

That drug that made me feel anything was possible,

I was capable of everything.

The drug that completed me and destroyed me.

That drug that made me feel so happy, so sad, so mad.

The drug that made me feel toxic and essential

at the same time.

I've been free of you.

The only drug I've tried and needed to experience.

Cause after you, not even ecstasy can be called a drug.

I'm sober now, sober of you."

NO EXPECTATIONS

"I don't want something serious.

I don't want to be tied and slaved to something.

I want to be free.

I want to be me.

So let's just take it easy,

no expectations, and let it be."

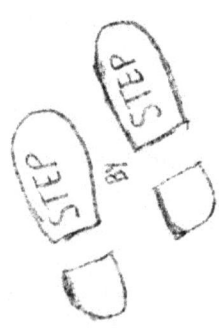

YOU CAME INTO MY LIFE

"You came into my life and brought light.

You came into my life and brought love.

You knocked on my door

and I opened it with just a bit of hope.

But there you were.

Making it impossible for me to back off.

I fell for your smile,

I fell for your kisses.

I fell for your soft touch

And your warm hugs.

I fell for you; slowly, entirely, just completely.

You made me feel strong,

You made me feel free.

You made me better,

Oh boy! You made me sweet.

You came into my life and brought color.

You came into my life and brought sense.

In fact, you came into my life and made me remember,

what life was really like."

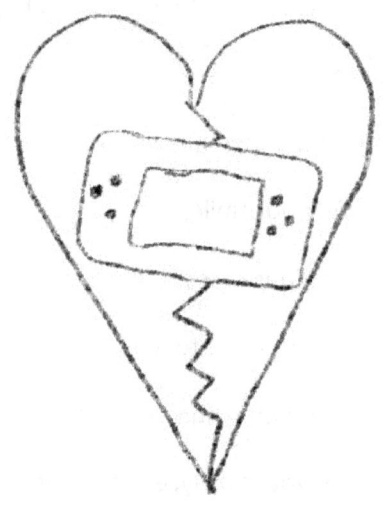

DON'T COME

"I loved you, you liked me.

I accepted who you were,

you loved having me.

I tried to stay, you opt to leave.

Oh honey, don't come begging,

I'm happily free."

THIS TIME

"And this time I said I'd be different.

No more text messages,

no more waiting on phone calls.

I'm not going to expect anything,

because I don't want to be disappointed.

Whatever happens, happens.

If I am special, you'll show it.

If you want me, you'll let me see it.

If you care enough, you'll make me change into that girl

that gave everything without expecting

nothing in return."

I TRUSTED YOU

"I trusted you.

I gave you my body,

I gave you my time.

Although I was slowly waiting for you to say goodbye.

I got too comfortable with you.

I liked your strengths,

I accepted your flaws.

But at the end,

you disappeared without a doubt."

AS IT IS

"I am too hurt for love.

I am too reserved for just sex.

I want to be seen, I want to be felt.

I want who touches my body to do it with respect.

You don't have to love me or pretend.

Just show me I am special,

and treat me as I deserve.

We are not fuck buddies,

We don't have to be best friends.

Just don't play with my heart

and waste my time,

and I'll keep you warm and treat you right."

SIGNING UP TO PLAY

"And let this be a game.

Who calls or texts first; who misses the most.

But there are rules that should be followed.

Don't fall, don't need, don't love.

Just play the game, enjoy the time.

Use all your best cards, and play smart.

At the end, it doesn't matter if you win or lose,

 because you got to participate.

And again, you knew you were signing up to play."

I NEEDED MORE

"And if you leave me today,

I feel I still needed a little more time.

One last dance,

one more soft kiss,

one last poem to write you,

one more movie to watch together.

I needed more days to prove you how much I love you.

But I guess if you didn't see that before,

then you don't deserve it.

And I shouldn't ask you to stay."

LOVING SOMEONE

"And the thing about loving someone is

that you're always afraid to lose them.

You live on the verge.

You give your all and question if it's good enough.

You're afraid one morning you'll wake up

and love isn't mutual anymore.

You're afraid to give too much and scare them away.

You're afraid to get hurt.

But you can't love someone this way.

Love is about giving.

So give your all and expect it's good enough.

If it's the right person, they will stay."

WORSE THAN A BROKEN HEART

"People always say 'you broke my heart'.

And even though I feel broken

and would probably never get fixed,

you didn't break my heart.

I still love myself, I still love this world.

I can say 'you fucked my mind.'

You have made me doubt every man in my life.

You gave me trust issues, insecurities,

and made me into a stone woman.

You didn't break my heart.

You broke my mind.

You gave me the power to let my mind

decide not to love.

And that right there,

is worse than a broken heart."

REMEMBER ME

"And if you get tired of me,

think about how it all started.

How we were before all this bullshit.

In love and crazy for each other.

Not giving a fuck about the world.

How we were before we started to fade away.

To change into this cold cycle called monotony.

We were happy, we were free.

No expectations that lead to disappointments.

No regrets, nothing to win, nothing to lose.

Just remember who we were.

Remember why you loved me and it will all make sense.

You'll get tired, we'll fade away…

But please, please, remember me,

before you forget."

WE LIKE THE PAIN

"Why is it that we always love those

who don't love us back?"

We give our all and receive nothing;

but yet continue to do it.

Do we like the pain?

Or do we just like to hold on to things

hoping they will change?

We like to fix things.

But sometimes by trying to fix those

who don't want to get fixed,

we end up breaking ourselves.

And at the end, there's no one to fix us."

UNTIL IT HURTS TOO MUCH

"People always tell others: "*I don't get why you stay.*'

And I was one of them.

But you see, no one can actually say that

without being in your position.

There are days I ask myself,

'why am I even here?'

But then I would never forget myself if I leave.

When you love someone who is fucked up,

it fucks you up.

There is nothing you can do about it.

You stay until you legit can't continue anymore.

And it hurts, yeah it fucking hurts.

It destroys you, it changes you.

But it makes you strong.

There is no way you are leaving

when everyone tells you to.

You are leaving when your hearts screams: '*SAVE ME.*'

And maybe everything will be worth it,

or maybe everyone else was right

and you were just love blind."

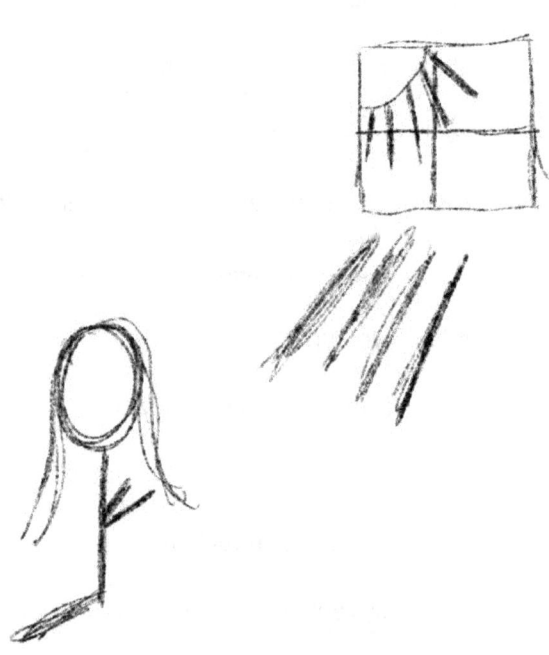

CUTE POEMS SUCK

"I don't write cute happy poems. What is the need?

Life is not fair or clean.

Love is dirty. It hurts, it stings.

So I'm not going to sit down and waste cute words

that can be much simpler.

I want to say I love you.

For who you are and who you make me be.

I love you for making me crazy,

for making me cry.

Love you for making me mad

and then giving this a try.

And even though we are fucked up and nuts,

I love you.

You make cruel reality be nice

and fake love poems sound lame

for not understanding how love is pain."

CAN'T LIE ABOUT THAT

"I didn't lie.

Everything I said, I meant.

Everything I did, was real.

We were complicated.

We had dreams of becoming something

we both knew we couldn't.

I didn't lie.

I guess we could say I kept some things.

I didn't express fully how I felt.

We pretended to be happy, we pretended to be

something we were not.

And I hid my emotions and thoughts from you.

I didn't lie.

I preferred to follow your game,

to make you happy.

And now you are mad at me because all this time,

I've been the only one falling.

I didn't lie. In fact, I can't lie.

I can't pretend all this time has meant nothing to me.

I can't be you. I can't lie so well.

I thought our dreams would become reality.

I thought what we had was love.

But I guess now days, people even lie about that.

THANK YOU LOVE

"Love sucks.

It hurts, it drains, it kills.

It takes everything from you.

It leaves you empty and confused.

Love is painful.

It takes the best of you.

It ruins you.

It makes you have hope on things

that will never come back.

Love is rude.

But life without love is stupid.

Love moves us.

I am who I am because of love.

So thank you love.

By ruining me, you made me stronger.

You made me real."

TO THE BEST ACTOR

"Acting has been my profession for years.

And today I have to say, I am impressed.

I met a great actor. Someone who truly knows

how to use his skills.

I met him over the summer.

A nice boy who seemed different than the rest.

So polite, kind, and warm.

He was a gentleman.

Over the years I got to know him,

and with time fall in love with him.

He was complicated, as all actors are,

 but he was always there.

I opened my heart to him and let him enter.

Soon after, I realized the show was over.

Once he had me, the audience he carried was gone.

 His amazing act was done.

Is Mejor to say ADIOS

Oh boy, I've never seen such talent.

To be able to hold a character for that long.

To pretend to love, to feel, to care.

They say acting is easy, but what this boy did

was unbelievable.

He acted out this perfect life we would once have,

and left me broken believing his act.

He was good. He was a great one.

I need to be more like him.

Pretend I am fine,

while I'm dying inside, thanks to him."

CAN'T BE FRIENDS

"How can I look you in the eyes and pretend

I don't see myself in them?

How can I touch your hand and pretend

mine doesn't belong in it?

How can I feel your skin

and pretend it doesn't warmth me?

How can I be your friend

and pretend I don't love you anymore?

Tell me how.

Because my body doesn't get used to it,

my heart rejects it, and my brain can't accept it."

HOPE IN THIS LOVE

"I still think we can work out.

There was so much love between us,

it is impossible to just disappear.

There was so much passion within us,

it isn't real to just fade away.

I know you love me. I know you still care.

I also know you are hurt and you are damn stubborn.

So now we are stuck.

Stuck in this weird stage of letting go and holding on.

And it hurts even more.

We can either grow together or destroy each other.

But I still believe in us, I just can't do it alone."

DECIDE

"Loving someone is not a game.

You can't put someone on hold or layaway.

You either have me or you don't.

I am tired of your '*I don't know*' or your "*I'm not ready*.'

I am not a dog who waits for their owner.

I am not a toy waiting to get picked.

If I put my time and effort, it's because I want you,

and if you don't do the same, it's because you don't.

So I need you to stop pretending

and start demonstrating.

I'm not here forever.

I have a heart, and it's getting tired."

WON'T BE THAT GIRL

"It's true.

People say you have to fight for what you want

and to not give up.

But there is a limit to that.

I can't fight for what isn't mine.

I can't want you if you have someone else.

I bet it makes you feel good, but here I am

asking myself a thousand questions on

why I'm not good enough.

And here I am being stupid on the fact that

I should know that I am.

I don't have to fight for something

it's not worth fighting for.

If you wanted me from the beginning,

you would've shown me.

So I'm sorry 'bro'.

I won't be that girl.

I won't beg you to choose me

because I'm not an option.

I've reached my limit."

YOU MADE IT WORSE

"I was in the dark and then you came in slowly.

It was like a door with light started to open

and then just closed.

Fast and hard.

And now it's worse.

I'm left in the dark waiting on the door

without knowing where to search for.

I'm lost.

I had hopes that are crushed now.

You shouldn't have opened that door.

You shouldn't have let me see the light.

You're gone now and it's darker than ever."

I DID CARE

"All this time I thought I wasn't enough,

that you needed more and that's why you searched in

other places for what I didn't have.

All this time I thought I didn't make you happy

and you needed other girls to make you laugh.

But all this time I was wrong.

I was too much.

How can I make someone happy

who's not happy with himself?

How can I make someone love me

who doesn't love himself?

You weren't searching for love in all those places.

You were searching for yourself.

And even though I love you,

I'm not a game.

I've found myself already and

I've been waiting too long for you.

Keep trying with them,

I wish you the best."

HE DIDN'T DESERVE IT

"Sometimes we give too much.

We give our all and expect nothing back.

We offer our hearts like it's something simple.

We become happy through the happiness

of that person. Everything we do is around them.

Our time, is their time.

Our space, is their space.

And there is nothing wrong with that.

It is beautiful to open up and feel.

But it is painful, it is horrible,

when we give too much to that person

that cares too little.

When you give your all, you give it away.

And when that person leaves, he takes it with him.

And that is the end of the story. Nothing left.

Not everybody deserves your all.

He really didn't."

QUESTIONS IN MY MIND

"Looking back at my life I wonder.

I wonder and question when did everything changed.

I remember us being so happy, so alive.

And now we're dead.

We are fading away.

But it makes me think if it was me.

Am I responsible for all of this?

Was I the only one who had hopes in this?

Was I the one who gave you everything?

Was I the one too blind to miss all the signs?

Were you always this cold?

I wanted us to be happy and got confused with the idea

and not the truth. And now I'm left alone.

Looking back at a lie that we created to survive.

You were never in love.

You got what you needed and continued with your life."

FOR A BEAUTIFUL GIRL

"It is not your fault.

Don't ever think you weren't good enough,

sexy enough, worthy enough, because you are.

The fact that you gave your all and he still left,

doesn't mean it's you. You are great.

You can't change a coward.

You are too much for him.

He runs away because he is not ready.

He is still immature and not brave enough.

He goes from body to body searching for himself.

He's afraid to commit. You don't need that man.

You are ready. You are brave, you are mature.

You are not afraid to loose and get hurt.

So sure, you'll cry now that he's gone.

But soon after you'll realize you need a man

and not a boy.

It is not your fault; he just needs to grow up."

YOU DESERVE TO BE SEEN

"All this time you've been questioning

what you did wrong.

You've been giving your all to someone

and receiving nothing in return.

He's been your priority; you've been an option.

But it is not your fault. You've been giving your body

and soul to someone who searches every week

in other bodies for himself. Someone who's afraid

to commit and terrified to be alone.

And you can't do that to yourself.

You can't be an in-between, a maybe.

It is not your fault that he is still finding himself.

But you can't wait around. You can't be an option.

You still have some work to do in yourself as well,

but you are ready to open up.

He is hurting you and you deserve more.

You deserve to be seen, not put on hold."

SAVE YOURSELF

"Stop lying to yourself.

Stop giving him the benefit of the doubt.

Deep down you know the truth.

If a man wants you, he'll do everything for you.

If he doesn't, he won't.

His no calls, no shows, speak for themselves.

His lack of attention, his disloyalty, say it all.

So I beg you, stop lying to yourself.

Stop believing his excuses.

You are better than a few hours of pleasure

and endless nights of loneliness.

Tonight you are your own savior.

Tonight you say stop.

Your happiness lays within you.

Your freedom has always been there.

Don't let him break you, don't give him that power.

You are hurting, but you can still be saved.

You are your hero tonight.

Time to forget this guy."

TAKES TIME

"I am being calm.

I am healing and trying to forget,

but you have to cut me some slack here.

I can't be okay all of a sudden because you left me

all of a sudden.

You vanished. Gone.

And I know you still care and want me to see it.

But we can't be cool, at least for now.

And I am glad that you're happy.

But it does kill me that it's not with me.

It takes some time to move on

and it takes more time when the one you love

 has already done it.

One day we'll smile and remember all this,

but not yet.

It'll take me some time from being an ex to a friend."

DON'T BELIEVE EVERYTHING

"And yes it is true what people say on the streets.

You left me.

You were the one that got away.

And probably it is true what people talk about.

They say you hurt me and destroyed me.

But I've heard some lies too.

I heard you broke me and I'm not fine.

And those lies I want to clarify.

You see, when you left, you opened my eyes.

You made me see everything I needed to see.

You made me realize how powerful and beautiful I am.

How talented I am.

How much I can love.

And even though all I gave, I never received back,

I am okay with that.

Is Mejor to say ADIOS

I understand that people say what they want to say.

And people leave when they want to leave.

And all we have are memories and experiences

that make us stronger.

So yes, you can believe you hurt me.

But don't believe I won't be okay

because step by step I am.

People come and go from your life.

Those who stay are the real ones.

I'm too old for fake people.

Too tired for half loves.

I want it all.

And it's okay if I have to wait for that.

I rather do that and get what I deserve.

So, thank you for making me see that.

I guess past lovers are essential.

You can let people know about this too."

PAIN

"Pain is part of life.

It makes us strong,

It makes us better.

Most of the time we avoid it.

We live running away from it.

But sometimes it's good to face it,

Look at pain in the eye and say:

I see you, I feel you, and I appreciate you.

It's good to face your demons.

When we do, we are invincible.

Don't let pain or anyone who causes it, ruin you.

Go face that battle.

I want to see you win."

YOU FIRST

"The problem is that sometimes we search in others

for things we'll find in ourselves.

We want others to love us in a way

we can only love ourselves.

This is when disappointment comes.

We cannot expect others to love and treat us in a way

we don't even treat ourselves.

We have to do that first.

As cliché as it sounds,

loving and accepting yourself will help others love you.

It's okay to be broken.

But it is not okay to ask someone to pick up the pieces

that you don't even have yet.

Look for those missing pieces.

Put them together.

Give yourself your all

and then watch the magic happen.

Others will love you even more."

PAIN II

"Some say is relative.

Some say it's bad.

I say it's good.

Pain makes you learn, makes you grow.

You see everything is a process.

And I'm processing a lot right now.

I appreciate pain.

It means it's real.

I still feel.

And even though it hurts, it's beautiful.

I am alive, and that means a lot.

Love the pain.

It's way better than not feeling anything.

It'll get better.

For now, just embrace it.

Accept it, and feel it.

Got to love pain."

CYCLES

"Is it all just a cycle?

Do we love, break, and recover?

We keep losing parts of ourselves in others.

We learn lessons. We gain memories.

But it still hurts.

You still question yourself every-time.

So, is life a cycle?

Are we bound to give our all to others

and feel emptier each time?

Is it okay to get tired?

What if there's nothing else to give?

Is that still okay?

If life is a cycle, I hope mine changes soon.

The only cycle I want is me giving my all

and you giving yours back over and over again.

I think most of the time is one sided

and that's why we are here tired of it.

Isn't easier if we both fight, grow, love,

and learn together?

I don't want to break no more.

Let's fall in love but together.

I'm tired of doing all the work.

Let's change the narrative.

Let's break the cycle."

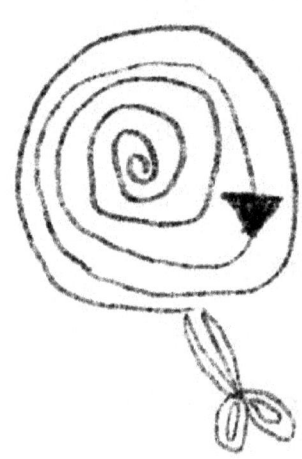

NO PERSON

"And there's always that one person.

That friend that turns his back.

That lover that breaks your heart.

That stranger that ruins your day.

Too many times we find ourselves giving that person

the power of changing us.

Of getting in the middle of who we are,

who we are meant to be.

But that person has no right.

No right or power to change you.

You are great.

And the only person you should listen to is yourself.

Deep down you know your worth.

You know your value.

And no person can take that away."

SHUT DOWN

"I loved you at your worst.

And you still left me.

I gave you my all

and you still walked away.

Every day I question:

Why wasn't I enough?

What did I do wrong?

But time has taught me that it wasn't me.

I did everything I could.

I gave you my all.

You were empty.

My job was not to fix you.

And by trying to,

I broke myself.

Is Mejor to say ADIOS

You needed to go.

It was time for another pitstop

to fill your emptiness in a different town.

This gas station shut down."

Pieces & Memories.

"That's what it's all about.

We leave pieces of ourselves in every lover.

We take pieces of them each time.

We feel empty, we feel full.

We gain memories that last

and others we want to forget.

We lose time and energy.

It's all a back and forth.

A win or lose.

But in this crazy game of life,

we always have pieces and memories.

Even when I'm broken,

I'm a better version of myself.

I've lost a lot of pieces of me.

I've gained a lot of memories.

And perhaps, when the time is right,

there will be a lover who will fill those empty spots

and give me endless memories

without taking a single piece of me ever again.

If you have found yours, cherish that,

because that is gold."

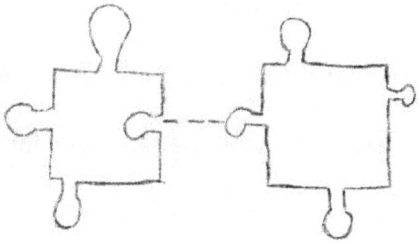

FAKE

"*Sweet*. He said he was sweet while his bitter

and sour touch would burn every part of my body.

Nice. He said he was nice, while every violent gesture

broke me down each day.

Good. He said he was good, while every bad trait of him

destroyed my spirit for months.

At the end, he was nothing he said he was.

He was a nightmare that lived rent free

in my body, mind, and soul.

A memory so dark that dimmed my light for so long.

Don't believe the words he says. Wait for actions.

Never believe a boy who calls himself a great man.

He was great, but just at *lying*."

FINAL WORDS

"I do love you.

I love you with my whole heart.

But I love myself more, so *goodbye*."

ABOUT THE AUTHOR

Alondra Delgado was born in Mayaguez, Puerto Rico. In her early years she started to show interest in acting by acting out scenes of Telenovelas. She began her acting career doing theater at four years old. After her first leading role in a Feature Film when she was seven years old, she fell in love with the art of storytelling and decided that acting was her passion and would be her profession. During her childhood she would spent most of her time writing poems and songs about love. She was often considered very "dramatic" and "passionate". Once she graduated High School, her and her family moved all the way to Los Angeles, California where Alondra completed her Bachelor's Degree in Acting for Film. After a couple of years Delgado started to make her dreams reality by getting casted for multiple TV Shows and Feature Films. Having completed many of her goals in the acting industry, Alondra decided to pursue her second passion which has always been writing. After many years of self-doubt she decided to put her doubts aside and believe in herself. Is Mejor to say ADIOS is the compilation of Alondra's poems for more than ten years. Poems related to personal events that made her who she is now. With this first book, Alondra has opened her heart to the world in the hopes of inspiring and touching other's hearts through writing. Because in her darkest days, these poems saved her. She hopes it can do the same for you.

www.ingramcontent.com/pod-product-compliance
Lightning Source LLC
Chambersburg PA
CBHW070204100426
42743CB00013B/3049